MATHS & ENGLISH FOR
AUTOMOTIVE

Graduated exercises and practice exam

Andrew Spencer and Jim Scivyer

Australia • Brazil • Japan • Korea • Mexico • Singapore • Spain • United Kingdom • United States

Maths & English for Automotive,
Andrew Spencer and Jim Scivyer

Publishing Director: Linden Harris
Publisher: Lucy Mills
Development Editor: Claire Napoli
Production Editor: Alison Cooke
Production Controller: Eyvett Davis
Marketing Manager: Lauren Mottram
Typesetter: Cenveo Publisher Services
Cover design: HCT Creative

© 2013, Cengage Learning EMEA

For product information and technology assistance, contact **emea.info@cengage.com**.

For permission to use material from this text or product, and for permission queries, email **emea.permissions@cengage.com**.

This work is Adapted from Pre Apprenticeship: Maths & Literacy Series by Andrew Spencer, published by Cengage Learning Australia Pty Limited © 2010.

British Library Cataloguing-in-Publication Data
A catalogue record for this book is available from the British Library.

ISBN: 978-1-4080-7738-2

Cengage Learning EMEA
Cheriton House, North Way, Andover, Hampshire, SP10 5BE, United Kingdom

Cengage Learning products are represented in Canada by Nelson Education Ltd.

For your lifelong learning solutions, visit
www.cengage.co.uk

Purchase your next print book, e-book or e-chapter at
www.cengagebrain.com

Printed in Malta by Melita Press
1 2 3 4 5 6 7 8 9 10 – 15 14 13

Maths & English for Automotive

Contents

Introduction

It has always been important to understand, from a teacher's perspective, the nature of the maths and English skills students need for their future, rather than teaching them textbook mathematics.

This has been a guiding principle behind the development of the content in this workbook. To teach maths and English that is *relevant* to students seeking apprenticeships is the best that we can do, to give students an education in the field that they would like to work in.

The content in this resource is aimed at the level that is needed for a student to have the best possibility of improving their maths and English skills specifically for the Automotive industry. Students can use this workbook to prepare for their functional skills assessment, or even to assist with basic maths and English for their Automotive qualification. This resource has the potential to improve the students' understanding of basic mathematical concepts that can be applied to the motor trade and garage environment. These resources have been trialled, and they work.

Commonly used industry terms are introduced so that students have a basic understanding of terminology they will encounter in the workplace environment. Students who can complete this workbook and reach a higher outcome in all topics will have achieved the goal of this resource.

The content in this workbook is the first step towards bridging the gap between what has been learnt in previous years, and what needs to be remembered and re-learnt for use in exams and in the workplace. Students will significantly benefit from the consolidation of the basic maths and English concepts.

In many ways, it is a win-win situation, with students enjoying and studying relevant maths and English for Automotive and training organizations and employers receiving students that have improved basic maths and English skills.

All that is needed is patience, hard work, a positive attitude, a belief in yourself that you can do it and a desire to achieve. The rest is up to you.

About the author

Andrew Spencer has studied education both within Australia and overseas. He has a Bachelor of Education, as well as a Masters of Science in which he specialized in teacher education. Andrew has extensive experience in teaching secondary mathematics throughout New South Wales and South Australia for well over 15 years. He has taught a range of subject areas, including Maths, English, Science, Classics, Physical Education and Technical Studies. His sense of the importance of practical mathematics has continued to develop with the range of subject areas he has taught in.

This workbook has been adapted by Jim Scivyer. Jim is a curriculum manager in the automotive engineering school at the College of North West London. He served his apprenticeship and worked for many years on Rolls Royce and Bentley motors. With extensive experience in manufacturer technical training, Jim worked as a senior technical trainer for Robert Bosch and then for Renault UK as Manager for the delivery of technical update training to the UK dealer network.

Acknowledgements

Andrew Spencer:
For Paula, Zach, Katelyn, Mum and Dad.
    Many thanks to Mal Aubrey (GTA) and all training organizations for their input.
    To the De La Salle Brothers for their selfless work with all students.
    Thanks also to Dr Pauline Carter for her unwavering support of all maths teachers.
    This is for all students who value learning, who are willing to work hard and who have character …
and are characters!

Jim Scivyer:
    For my wife and best friend Hayley. My fantastic children Roy, Grace and Richard. My Mum, Dad and brother Chris.

ENGLISH

Unit 1: Spelling

Short-answer questions

Specific instructions to students

- This is an exercise to help you identify and to correct spelling errors.
- Read the activity below, then answer accordingly.

Read the following passage and identify and correct the spelling errors.

A Ford Foccus is brought into a garage for a Magor service. The car needs 2 wiper blades replased as well as a new door mirror. In addision, the tracking needs to be checked, the suspension needs a complete rebuild and the cost of Labar is one of the main costs. The service managor wants the job completed by noon. The apprentice replaces all of the parts and then uses the wheel alignment equipment to complete the job.

After lunch, a Vauxhall Astra has a damiged door that has to be removed and repared. To do this, the apprentise sprays the nuts with WD40 then uses a soket set, with a 14 mm socket to remove the nuts. The job card also indikated that the window has to be taken out. Several deep skratches are on the window and a new one has to be put in. The work must be complated by the end of the day. The apprentice finds rust at the base of the door and asks the service managar wether it should be cut out.

Incorrect words:

_____

_____

Correct words:

_____

_____

Unit 2: Grammar and Punctuation

Short-answer questions

Specific instructions to students

- The following questions will help you practise your grammar and punctuation.
- Read the following questions, then answer accordingly.

QUESTION 1

Which linking word or phrase could you use instead of 'whereas'?

Answer

QUESTION 2

What does the linking word 'alternatively' mean?

Answer

QUESTION 3

What punctuation is missing from the following sentence?

A full range of services including inspection and repair of all makes of vehicle computer diagnostics air conditioning service and tyre check and replacement are available from this garage.

Answer

QUESTION 4

What is wrong with the following text? Correct the following sentences.

Last Saturday the garage was extremely busy; grace was run off her feet with all the customers that had been booked in. grace was pleased that she had remembered to ask tom to come in to help. She had felt a bit guilty as she had had to ask tom to travel in from manchester, where he had been on a stag do the night before.

Answer

QUESTION 5

When you have completed a section of writing, what should you look for when checking through your work?

Answer

QUESTION 6

What is wrong with the following text?

Why not visit our new luxury car showroom set in the heart of rural Lancashire? Youre sure to receive a warm welcome, and be shown the latest models of luxury sports cars we have available. All cars are available to test drive with our experienced sales team. To find out more or book an appointment, call Andrew on 01435 778367.

Answer

QUESTION 7

Can you identify the mistake in this job application letter?

Dear Madam

I wish to apply for the vacancy of sales advisor at your Vauxhall dealership, as advertised in this week's Gloucester Globe.

I have just completed my Level 2 NVQ Diploma in Light Vehicle Maintenance course at Dinsdale Park Colleage and am now looking for work in the Gloucester area.

I enclose a copy of my CV and look forward to hearing from you.

Yours faithfully,

Luke Smith

Answer

QUESTION 8

Can you identify the mistake in this advert?

> **The Body Repair to Go, West London**
>
> Body Repair to Go is set in West London and is your one stop shop for vehicle or accident repairs. At Body Repair to Go your car will be treeted like a baby and handled with care. All car resprays/bodywork is painstakingly carried out to remove dents, rust, scratches and scuffs. Please ring 0151 629 40276 to find out more about our special services.

Answer

Answer

QUESTION 9

Add commas to the following text to make the sense clearer.

> Cleaning an oil spill is a very simple task when done correctly. An oil spillage can be very dangerous someone could easily slip on the oil or if there is a large amount it could also be a fire hazard. Spillages should be cleaned up as soon as they happen a small amount of oil can easily be soaked up with an absorbent cloth. If a large oil spillage occurs you should soak it up with absorbent granules.
>
> Allow them to soak in for a few hours. When the oil has soaked in sweep the granules up and treat them as hazardous waste. They should be stored until you have a large amount and then be collected by a specialist waste company for correct disposal. If the floor still has a greasy feel use some diluted detergent and mop the floor then allow to dry.

Short-answer questions

Specific instructions to students

- These exercises will help you understand what you read.
- Read the following activities, then answer the questions that follow.

Comprehension Task 1

Read the following passage and answer the questions in sentence form.

Bill the garage owner had a busy Monday to deal with. He clocked in at 7.45 a.m. and he knew the day would not be an easy one. One mechanic was off sick and he had several big jobs booked in. When Jed, the new apprentice, arrived Bill got him to work straight away. A Ford Focus needed a major service, while a Vauxhall Astra needed the brakes removed and inspected. Later, Jed found that all four brake discs needed machining. Another mechanic, Dave, started dismantling the handbrake assembly on a Renault Laguna which took him close to 45 minutes due to a broken cable. Chris started changing the transmission oil on an Range Rover which didn't take too long. The day got busier after that. By the time Bill clocked out at 5 p.m., he was looking forward to heading home and putting his feet up.

QUESTION 1

Why did Bill think that the day was going to be a busy one?

Answer:

QUESTION 2

What was the first job that Jed needed to start?

Answer:

QUESTION 3

What was the problem that Jed found after he had inspected the brakes?

Answer:

QUESTION 4

Why did Dave take longer than expected on removing the brake cable?

Answer:

QUESTION 5

How long was Bill's work day?

Answer:

Comprehension Task 2

Read the following passage and answer the questions in sentence form.

Sam was an apprentice technician and fairly new to his role. He liked to get into work early at 7.30am, and this morning was no exception, even though the first customer was not booked in until the garage opened at 8.30 a.m.

His manager, Robert, had left him a list of jobs that needed to be done, but he was not sure whether any of the jobs required immediate attention or if they were of equal importance. Robert liked him to keep occupied while he was not busy helping out other colleagues in the garage. He checked with his manager to find out which jobs needed doing first, then prioritized the jobs and ticked them off as he carried them out. Robert was busy for most of the day interviewing for a new foreman to join the team.

While Sam was carrying out these jobs, he was asked by his colleagues to carry out duties. Helen, the senior technician, asked him to raise her customer's car onto the 4-post ramp ready for starting her inspection of the under body of the vehicle. He also washed the cars after each of her three MOTs were completed in the morning, before she left for the afternoon, to go to a hospital appointment. Sam managed to take a 15 minute break between helping Helen with her customers' cars and sweeping the garage floor.

He found that ticking off jobs as he completed them was really helpful, as he had to keep stopping so he could attend to requests from colleagues. Steve, another technician, wanted him to prepare a trolley of tools for a wheel replacement and locate the correct replacement wheel. Steve asked Sam to help remove and replace the wheel, once the vehicle was raised using the jack.

Later on in the afternoon, Sam also helped out on reception, as the receptionist had gone home sick at 2.00 p.m. He welcomed customers, completed their job cards, and offered them refreshments for those waiting for their vehicles to be repaired. He answered the telephone and took appointments, checking first with Steve that he had taken the correct details and got the right appointment times. It was lucky that he had managed to eat his lunch between 1.00-1.30 p.m.; otherwise it would have been difficult to take a break.

As the last few customers came into the garage to collect their fixed cars, Sam managed a quick break of 10 minutes. When he returned, he tidied the reception area, helped tidy away the tools into the correct places, took out the garage waste for collection and swept the floors ready for the next day. It had been a long day, but he had enjoyed the variety of jobs that the day had brought. All the staff finished work at the garage at 5.30 p.m. and left to go home.

QUESTION 1

How many cars did Sam wash for Helen?

Answer:

QUESTION 2

Who replaced the wheel on Steve's customer's car?

Answer:

QUESTION 3

Sam started work at 7.30 a.m. and finished work at 5.30 p.m.; how much time did he take for breaks and lunch?

Answer:

QUESTION 4

What was the manager occupied with for the majority of the day?

Answer:

QUESTION 5

Why did Sam only check with Steve, when making appointments?

Answer:

QUESTION 6

What evidence is there of Sam planning and managing his workload?

Answer:

Unit 4: Formal Letter Writing Skills

Short-answer questions

Specific instructions to students

- These exercises will help you practise writing formal letters.
- Read the following information on formal letter writing, then write your own letters following the instructions provided.

A formal letter is a method of communication that uses a professional tone and manner. There are many reasons for writing a formal letter. It could be to order supplies, to identify a mistake that was committed or to apologize for an error. A formal letter should be clear, concise and courteous as well as following a set structure. This should include:

1. The sender's address.

2. Name, title and company name.

3. Date (day, month and year).

4. Heading to indicate the reason for writing the letter.

5. Greeting (Dear Mr/Mrs).

6. Introductory paragraph.

7. Middle paragraphs containing the relevant information behind writing the letter.

8. Closing paragraph describing what action you expect the recipient to take and a courteous closing sentence.

9. A complimentary close (Yours faithfully if you do not know the recipient or Yours sincerely if you know the recipient).

10. Leave room for your signature.

Section A: Letter of complaint

You have recently purchased a new sound system for your car, from a well known parts and accessory supplier. Having spent many hours fitting it, you find that two of the speakers do not work properly and that there is an intermittent fault with the remote control unit. When you returned to the place where you bought it, the sales adviser was very dismissive of your concerns and refused to help you. Using the appropriate language, write a letter of complaint to the company's head office, setting out:

- what you purchased

- what is wrong with it

- how you were treated by the sales adviser

- what you would like the company to do to resolve your complaint.

Section B: Job application letter

Trainee Vehicle Technician / Car Mechanic Main Car Dealership

Location: Salisbury, Wiltshire

Salary: £14,000 – rising to £17,000 per annum on qualification

We are currently recruiting for a Trainee Motor Vehicle Technician / Motor Vehicle Mechanic who has commitment, ambition and a real desire to learn about a full range of vehicle diagnostics. Reporting to the Workshop Supervisor, the successful applicant will be part of a small team responsible for the repair and maintenance of a range of vehicles.

The successful applicant must have:

- A quality focus, taking pride in excellent workmanship
- Enthusiasm to work hard
- The ability to work as part of a team.

Please send your application to Mr Andrew Briars, Salisbury Motors, North Way, Salisbury, Wiltshire

---

You have seen the above advert in your local paper with a vacancy for a trainee. Write a letter of application, setting out why you would like the job and the skills that you have that make you suitable for the job. Continue writing your letter using the notes section at the back of this workbook if required.

Unit 5: Industry Related Writing Skills

Short-answer questions

Specific instructions to students

- These exercises will help you practise writing skills that you will need to use when working in the motor industry.
- Complete the writing exercises following the instructions provided.

Section A: Writing emails

Write an email to your customer, Mr Andrew Richardson, reminding him that his Transit van is due for a 60k service in 30 days time.

To:
Subject:
Message:

Section B: Completing a job card

Fill in all of the sections of this job card for a Volkswagen Golf TSI Registration GT07 GRX that has been booked in for a 30,000 mile service and replacement of the front and rear brake linings by the vehicle owner Mr Thomas Biggs of 73 Elm Road, Reading. The owner will only be available on his mobile during the day the work is carried out. His mobile phone number is 07853 384869.

CUSTOMER NAME: DATE: MILEAGE:

ADDRESS:

TEL HOME: TEL WORK:

VEHICLE MAKE: REGISTRATION:

MODEL: ENGINE NO:

CHASSIS NO:

WORK REQUIRED:

WORK CARRIED OUT:

PARTS USED:

ADDITIONAL REPAIRS REQUIRED:

INVOICE DATE: INVOICE NO:

Customer signature

Section C: Work carried out on a job card

When you write up a job card for the work that has been carried out on a customer's vehicle, it is important to give as much detail as possible. Otherwise the customer may not be charged for all of your work and you in turn could be paid less money.

QUESTION 1

A BMW Mini has had a full service, front and rear brakes and some suspension work. Give a full write up of the work carried out.

QUESTION 2

Give a full write up of the type of extra work that might be required when working on an older vehicle, where the job has not gone exactly to plan due to seized and worn components.

QUESTION 3

A Ford Focus has had a front end impact. Give a full write up of the work carried out.

QUESTION 4

A diesel powered Ford Transit van has had an engine rebuild. Give a full write up of the work carried out.

Section D: Completing a parts invoice

Complete this blank invoice for the 30,000 mile service and brake repairs that were carried out in the job card activity on the previous page. Give the customer a 10% discount and charge VAT at the current rate.

INVOICE

DATE:

INVOICE:

CUSTOMER ID:

BILL TO:

DESCRIPTION	AMOUNT
Items Not Subject to Sales Tax	
SUBTOTAL	
Items Not Subject to Sales Tax	
SUBTOTAL	
VAT RATE	%
TAX	
S&H	
OTHER	
TOTAL DUE	

OTHER COMMENTS

1. Total payment due in 10 days

2. Please include the invoice number on your cheque

Make all cheques payable to

If you have any questions about this invoice, please contact:

Thank You For Your Business!

Section A: Car descriptions

Select a supercar of your choice and write a full technical description of the vehicle. This should include vehicle layout, body style and the type of engine being used. If you are unsure of any of the details, ask your tutor before starting.

Answer:

Section B: Vehicle modification

Select a vehicle of your choice and write a full technical description of any modification that you would carry out to improve this car. This should include what you would do, how you would carry it out and your reasons for the modifications. If you are unsure of any of the details, ask your tutor before starting.

Answer:

Section C: Persuasive writing

You are placing an advert on an auction website to sell your car. Write a full and honest description, highlighting all of the good points that will persuade someone to bid on your item. Think carefully about:

- the tone and language you use to make your item sound appealing to potential customers.

- making sure your description is clear and concise.

- the use of fact and opinion in your description.

Answer:

Unit 7: Gathering and Presenting Data

Short-answer questions

Specific instructions to students

- This section is designed to help you to improve your ability to gather, present and interpret data appropriately.
- Read the following questions and answer all of them in the spaces provided.
- You will also need to use extra paper or a computer programme to create a spreadsheet.

Select 12 supercars of your choice.

QUESTION 1

Create a spreadsheet to display your list of cars.

a) Add extra columns and find each of the following:
- Price of the vehicle
- Top speed of the vehicle
- 0 to 60mph time

b) In the space below draw a pie chart to show vehicle price:
- Up to £100k
- £100k to £200k
- Over £200k

QUESTION 2

What conclusions can you draw from your pie chart?

_____

_____

_____

_____

_____

QUESTION 3

Describe the variation in the number of supercars that can accelerate from 0 to 60mph in less than 4 seconds. Include the fastest and slower cars in your description.

_____

_____

_____

QUESTION 4

Describe the variation in the price of the supercars. Include the most popular price bracket in your description.

_____

_____

_____

Unit 8: Different Types of Text

Section A: Comparing different types of text

Short-answer questions

Specific instructions to students

- This is an exercise to help you identify different types of text.
- Read the activity below, then answer accordingly.

Read each of the following paragraphs, state the purpose of each type of text, explain whether the text is formal or informal and why it is appropriate in this context.

Text A – Dave, can you pick up the parts for Tom's van and then go round to the paint shop to refit the bumper on the blue Fiesta. Thanx Raj

Purpose of text:

_____

_____

Formal/informal:

_____

Why the text is appropriate:

_____

_____

Text B – Place a small amount of engine oil onto the lip seal before pressing it into the casing, use special tool ST1034 for this operation. Once the seal is firmly in place, refit the end cover and tighten the securing bolts to the correct torque (see fig 008).

Purpose of text:

_____

_____

Formal/informal:

_____

Why the text is appropriate:

_____

_____

Text C – Please be advised that if this amount of money has not been paid in full, within 30 days of this notice, we will take legal proceedings to recover all of your outstanding debt.

Purpose of text:

_____

_____

Formal/informal:

_____

Why the text is appropriate:

_____

_____

Text D – Work carried out:

- 36,000 service
- Checked adjusted tracking
- Fitted new front brake pads.

Purpose of text:

_____

_____

Formal/informal:

_____

Why the text is appropriate:

_____

_____

Section B: Factual and subjective text

Short-answer questions

Specific instructions to students

- This is an exercise to help you identify factual and subjective text.
- Read the activity below, then answer the questions accordingly.

Text can either be factual or subjective.

If a piece of text is factual it is based on real evidence and records of events which is not biased by the writer's opinion.

If a piece of text is subjective, it contains an individual's personal perspective, feelings or opinions which might differ from another individual's view of the same subject.

Which of the following is fact and which is opinion?

QUESTION 1

Lewis Hamilton is the best racing driver that I have ever seen.

QUESTION 2

The 2012 World F1 Constructors' championship was won by the Red Bull team.

QUESTION 3

The Bugatti Veyron looks great in blue.

QUESTION 4

My car is really comfortable on a long journey.

QUESTION 5

Nissan make cars in a number of countries including the UK.

QUESTION 6

You must wear the appropriate PPE when you are spraying a car.

QUESTION 7

The letters PSV stand for Public Service Vehicle.

QUESTION 8

Buses look better when they are painted red.

QUESTION 9

Volkswagen make good quality cars.

QUESTION 10

Snap-on make tools for the motor trade.

QUESTION 11

Chrome spanners not only look good, they feel sturdy when you use them.

QUESTION 12

The Le Mans 24-hour endurance race is held in France.

Section C: Appropriate tone and language

Short-answer questions

Specific instructions to students

- This is an exercise to help you understand the appropriate tone and language to use in text.
- Read the activity below, then answer the question accordingly.

Re-write the below paragraph to make it more appropriate for its audience. Think specifically about the language, tone and purpose of the text.

For the manager of Top Mechanics Ltd.

Your mechanic did a bad job fixing my car. The brakes are still noisy and your mechanic was rude. He told me I was imagining the noise and wouldn't replace the brakes again. What your mechanic did was wrong and he was bang out of order. I will be coming back into your service department on Friday and you will be giving me my money back.

From
Thomas Smith

MATHEMATICS

It is important to show your workings out to indicate how you calculated your answer. Use this workbook to practise the questions and record your answers. Use extra paper if necessary to record your workings out.

Unit 9: General Mathematics

Short-answer questions

Specific instructions to students

- This unit will help you to improve your general mathematical skills.
- Read the following questions and answer all of them in the spaces provided.
- You may not use a calculator.
- You need to show all of your working out.

QUESTION 1

What unit of measurement would you use to measure:

a Spark plug gaps?

Answer:

_____

b The temperature of radiator coolant?

Answer:

_____

c The amount of oil in a transmission?

Answer:

_____

d The weight of a car body?

Answer:

_____

e The speed of a vehicle?

Answer:

_____

f The amount of oil in an unopened oil container?

Answer:

_____

g The cost of a second hand car?

Answer:

_____

QUESTION 2

Give an example of each of the following, and very briefly describe an instance of where they may be found in the automotive industry.

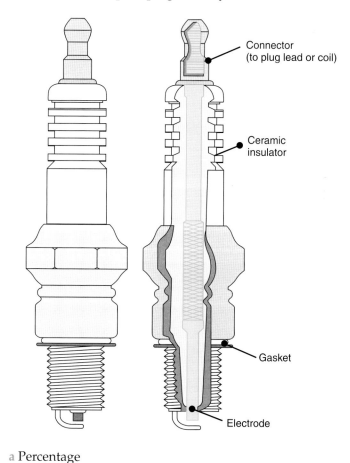

Spark plug cutaway

Connector (to plug lead or coil)

Ceramic insulator

Gasket

Electrode

a Percentage

Answer:

_____

b Decimal

Answer:

_____

c Fraction

Answer:

_____

d Mixed number

Answer:

_____

e Ratio

Answer:

_____

f Angle

Answer:

_____

QUESTION 3
Convert the following units:

a 12 kilograms to grams

Answer:

_____

b 4 tonnes to kilograms

Answer:

_____

c 120 centimetres to metres

Answer:

_____

d 1140 millilitres to litres

Answer:

_____

e 1650 grams to kilograms

Answer:

_____

f 1880 kilograms to tonnes

Answer:

_____

g 13 metres to centimetres

Answer:

_____

h 4.5 litres to millilitres

Answer:

_____

QUESTION 4
List the following in descending order:

0.4   0.04   4.1   40.0   400.00   4.0

Answer:

_____

QUESTION 5
Write the decimal number that is between the following:

a 0.2 and 0.4

Answer:

_____

b 1.8 and 1.9

Answer:

_____

c 12.4 and 12.6

Answer:

_____

d 28.3 and 28.4

Answer:

_____

e 101.5 and 101.7

Answer:

_____

QUESTION 6
Round off the following numbers to two (2) decimal places:

a 12.346

Answer:

_____

b 2.251

Answer:

_____

c 123.897

Answer:

_____

d 688.882

Answer:

_____

e 1209.741

Answer:

_____

QUESTION 7

Estimate the following by approximation:

a $1288 \times 19 =$

Answer:

b $201 \times 20 =$

Answer:

c $497 \times 12.2 =$

Answer:

d $1008 \times 10.3 =$

Answer:

e $399 \times 22 =$

Answer:

f $201 - 19 =$

Answer:

g $502 - 61 =$

Answer:

h $1003 - 49 =$

Answer:

i $10\,001 - 199 =$

Answer:

j $99.99 - 39.8 =$

Answer:

QUESTION 8

What do the following add up to?

a £4, £4.99 and £144.95

Answer:

b 8.75, 6.9 and 12.55

Answer:

c 65 ml, 18 ml and 209 ml

Answer:

d 21.3 g, 119 g and 884.65 g

Answer:

QUESTION 9

Subtract the following:

a 2338 from 7117

Answer:

b 1786 from 3112

Answer:

c 5979 from 8014

Answer:

d 11 989 from 26 221

Answer:

e 108 767 from 231 111

Answer:

QUESTION 10

Use division to solve the following:

a $2177 \div 7$

Answer:

b $4484 \div 4$

Answer:

c $63.9 \div 0.3$

Answer:

d $121.63 \div 1.2$

Answer:

e $466.88 \div 0.8$

Answer:

The following information is provided for Question 11.

To solve using BODMAS, in order from left to right, solve the Brackets first, then Of, then Division, then Multiplication, then Addition and lastly Subtraction. The following example has been done for your reference.

EXAMPLE:

Solve $(4 \times 7) \times 2 + 6 - 4$.

STEP 1

Solve the Brackets first: $(4 \times 7) = 28$

STEP 2

No Division so next solve Multiplication: $28 \times 2 = 56$

STEP 3

Addition is next: $56 + 6 = 62$

STEP 4

Subtraction is the last process: $62 - 4 = 58$

FINAL ANSWER:

58

QUESTION 11

Using BODMAS, solve:

a $(6 \times 9) \times 5 + 7 - 2$

Answer:

---

b $(9 \times 8) \times 4 + 6 - 1$

Answer:

---

c $3 \times (5 \times 7) + 11 - 8$

Answer:

---

d $5 \times (8 \times 3) + 9 - 6$

Answer:

---

e $7 + 6 \times 3 + (9 \times 6) - 9$

Answer:

---

f $6 + 9 \times 4 + (6 \times 7) - 21$

Answer:

Section A: Addition

Short-answer questions

Specific instructions to students

- This section will help you to improve your skills of addition for basic operations.
- Read the questions below and answer all of them in the spaces provided.
- You may not use a calculator.
- You need to show all of your working out.

QUESTION 1

To re-wire a 2 m × 1.5 m trailer, an auto electrician uses 2 m, 1 m, 3 m and 5 m of electrical wire. How much wire would be used in total?

Answer:

_____

QUESTION 2

To re-wire a caravan, an auto electrician may use 2.5 m, 1.8 m, 3.3 m and 15.2 m of electrical wire. How much electrical wire would be used in total?

Answer:

_____

QUESTION 3

A parts department stocks 127 top radiator hoses, 368 bottom radiator hoses and 723 various hoses. How many hoses do they have in stock in total?

Answer:

_____

QUESTION 4

A Ford Focus is driven 352 miles, 459 miles, 4872 miles and 198 miles. How far has the car been driven in total?

Answer:

_____

QUESTION 5

A courier driver uses the following amounts of diesel in May: 35.5 litres in week one, 42.9 litres in week two, 86.9 litres in week three and 66.2 litres in week four.

a How many litres have been used?

Answer:

_____

b If diesel costs £1.40 per litre, how much would fuel have cost for the month?

Answer:

QUESTION 6

If an apprentice mechanic buys an oil filter for £12.50, four spark plugs for £16.80 and a radiator hose for £6.75, how much has been spent in total?

Answer:

QUESTION 7

A mechanic uses 10 mm nuts to complete three jobs. If he uses 26 nuts on one job, 52 nuts on another job and 48 nuts on the last job, how many nuts has he used in total?

Answer:

QUESTION 8

A car enthusiast buys a new silencer for £125.80, a sound system for £466.99 and a new steering wheel for £88.50. How much has he spent altogether?

Answer:

QUESTION 9

A rally car driver travels 36.8 miles, 98.7 miles, 77.2 miles and 104.3 miles in four stages. What is his total distance covered?

Answer:

QUESTION 10

178 bolts, 188 nuts and 93 washers are needed to complete some mechanical work on a car. How many parts in total are needed?

Answer:

Section B: Subtraction

Short-answer questions

Specific instructions to students

- This section will help you to improve your subtraction skills for basic operations.
- Read the following questions and answer all of them in the spaces provided.
- You may not use a calculator.
- You need to show all of your working out.

QUESTION 1

A vehicle is filled up with petrol to its limit of 52 litres. If the driver uses 22 litres on one night, 17 litres on the next night and 11 litres on the third night, how much is left in the tank?

Answer:

QUESTION 2

If a driver covers 362 miles and another driver covers 169 miles, how much farther has the first driver gone than the second driver?

Answer:

QUESTION 3

In the same month, Truck Driver A uses 243.8 litres of LPG, and Truck Driver B uses 147.9 litres of LPG. How much more LPG does Truck Driver A use?

Answer:

QUESTION 4

A mechanic uses 39 nuts from a box that contains a total of 163 nuts. How many nuts will be left after the mechanic has used the nuts?

Answer:

QUESTION 5

A service on a car costs £224.65. The mechanic takes off a discount of approximately 10%, which is rounded off to £25.00. How much does the customer need to pay after the discount?

Answer:

QUESTION 6

Over the course of a year, an apprentice drives her motorbike 12,316 miles. Of this, 5787 miles is for her personal use. How many miles was used in travelling for work?

Answer:

QUESTION 7

A garage uses the following amounts of oil for three services:

Job 1: 5.5 litres

Job 2: 3.8 litres

Job 3: 6.9 litres

How much oil is left from a drum that contained 180 litres of oil to begin with?

Answer:

QUESTION 8

During one month, a mechanic replaces 74 spark plugs on several different cars. If there was a total of 132 spark plugs to begin with, how many are now left?

Answer:

QUESTION 9

A car odometer has a reading of 78,769 before a trip is made. Afterwards, it reads 84,231. How many miles have been travelled?

Answer:

QUESTION 10

A paint sprayer uses the following amounts of the same paint on three separate jobs:

Job 1: 8.7 litres

Job 2: 6.9 litres

Job 3: 15.3 litres

If there were 50 litres of paint in a drum to begin with, how much would be left?

Answer:

Section C: Multiplication

Short-answer questions

Specific instructions to students

- This section will help you to improve your multiplication skills for basic operations.
- Read the following questions and answer all of them in the spaces provided.
- You may not use a calculator.
- You need to show all of your working out.

QUESTION 1

If a hybrid car travels at 60 mph, how far will it travel in 9 hours?

Answer:

QUESTION 2

If a car travels at 80 mph, how far will it travel in 3 hours?

Answer:

QUESTION 3

A courier uses 15 litres of fuel for one specific trip. How much fuel will he use if the same trip needs to be completed 26 times?

Answer:

QUESTION 4

On an automotive assembly line, a worker uses 12 nuts, 14 washers and eight bolts to secure one door panel. How many nuts, washers and bolts would be used on 144 door panels?

Answer:

QUESTION 5

On a production line, 1.5 m of green wire, 2.2 m of red wire and 0.8 m of yellow wire are used in the electrical system of one car. How much of each wire would be used for 39 cars?

Answer:

QUESTION 6

24 wheel nuts are used to secure four wheels onto one small car. How many nuts would you need for 87 cars?

Answer:

QUESTION 7

A car uses 9 litres of LPG for every 100 km. How much LPG would be used for 450 km?

Answer:

QUESTION 8

If a crash repairer's workshop used 273 nuts per month, how many would be used over a year?

Answer:

QUESTION 9

An auto electrician uses 3 m of wire every day. If there are 28 days in a typical month, how much wire does the auto electrician use in a typical month?

Answer:

QUESTION 10

If a car travels at 110 mph for 5 hours, how far has it travelled?

Answer:

Section D: Division

Short-answer questions

Specific instructions to students

- This section will help you to improve your division skills for basic operations.
- Read the following questions and answer all of them in the spaces provided.
- You may not use a calculator.
- You need to show all of your working out.

QUESTION 1

An auto electrician has a 24 m coil of wire. How many jobs can be completed if each standard job requires 3 m of wire?

Answer:

QUESTION 2

If a paint sprayer earns £668 for working a 5-day week, how much does the paint sprayer earn per day?

Answer:

QUESTION 3

A garage owner buys 14,000 litres of fuel in bulk. Each of the fuel drums contains 180 litres. How many drums can be filled? Any left over?

Answer:

QUESTION 4

A truck driver covers 780 miles in a 5-day week. On average, how many miles per day has been travelled?

Answer:

QUESTION 5

The total weight of a four-wheel car is 1288 kilograms. How much load, in kilograms, is on each wheel?

Answer:

QUESTION 6

An articulated truck covers 3925 miles over a 7-day period. How many miles are covered, on average, each day?

Answer:

QUESTION 7

At a yearly stock take, a storeperson counts 648 spark plugs. If there are six in each box, how many boxes are there?

Answer:

QUESTION 8

408 light bulbs are ordered in for a vehicle technician. If there are four in each box, how many boxes are there?

Answer:

QUESTION 9

A truck delivers 4644 tyres to a tyre centre. The tyres will be used for four-wheel cars only. How many cars could be fitted with tyres? Are any tyres left over?

Answer:

QUESTION 10

A driver travels 890 miles in 28 days. How many miles are travelled, on average, each day?

Answer:

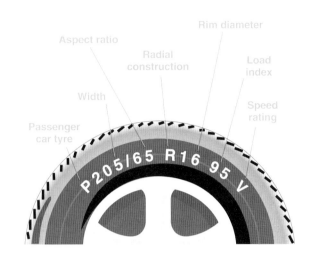

Section A: Addition

Short-answer questions

Specific instructions to students

- This section will help you to improve your skills of addition when working with decimals.
- Read the following questions and answer all of them in the spaces provided.
- You may not use a calculator.
- You need to show all of your working out.

QUESTION 1

If you buy a set of four new tyres for £416.88, and a spare retread tyre for £42.75, how much will be paid in total?

Answer:

_____

QUESTION 2

An auto technician buys a multimeter for £39.95, some wire for £29.95, several light bulbs for £44.55 and some clamps for £19.45. How much has been spent?

Answer:

_____

QUESTION 3

If the stem of one valve measures 99.85 mm and another stem of a valve measures 97.55 mm, what is the total length of the two valves?

Answer:

_____

QUESTION 4

One piston measures 10.205 cm and another is 8.438 cm. What is the total length?

Answer:

_____

QUESTION 5

A mechanic buys the following: a radiator hose for £8.99, a fan belt for £6.50, oil for £12.30 and a spare tyre for £65.90. What is the total cost?

Answer:

_____

QUESTION 6

If a truck driver travels 65.8 miles, 36.5 miles, 22.7 miles and 89.9 miles, how far has been travelled in total?

Answer:

_____

QUESTION 7

What is the total length of a screwdriver with a handle of 5.5 cm and an end of 7.8 cm?

Answer:

QUESTION 8

A gudgeon pin on a car has a diameter of 2.42 cm; another on a truck has a diameter of 3.79 cm. What is the total diameter?

Answer:

QUESTION 9

A mechanic completes three jobs. The first job totals £450.80, the second job totals £1130.65 and the last job totals £660.45. How much has been charged in total?

Answer:

QUESTION 10

A car's engine has a standard bore of 89.90 mm. If the car has four cylinders, find the total length of the four bores.

Answer:

Section B: Subtraction

Short-answer questions

Specific instructions to students

- This section will help you to improve your subtraction skills when working with decimals.
- Read the following questions and answer all of them in the spaces provided.
- You may not use a calculator.
- You need to show all of your working out.

QUESTION 1

A car enthusiast cuts the road springs on his car. If the springs measured 38.68 cm and he cuts 3.95 cm off, what length will they now be?

Answer:

QUESTION 2

If a crash repairer cuts off 22.5 cm from a length of metal stock that is 1.45 m long, how much is left?

Answer:

QUESTION 3

If a paint sprayer completes a job that costs £789.20 and then a discount of £75.50 is given, how much is the final cost?

Answer:

QUESTION 4

An apprentice works 38 hours and earns £245.60. £48.85 is used for petrol and oil. How much of her earnings are left?

Answer:

QUESTION 5

A jack is raised under a car to a height of 65.60 cm. It is then lowered by 8.95 cm. What height is it at?

Answer:

QUESTION 6

If one piston has a diameter of 9.50 cm and another has a diameter of 8.85 cm, what is the difference between the two?

Answer:

QUESTION 7

A spark plug gap on a new plug is 32.50 mm; the gap on a worn plug is 32.85 mm. What is the difference?

Answer:

QUESTION 8

A panel beater has a 4Kg can of filler. It is used on three different jobs: 285 g for job 1, 560 g for job 2 and 1.3Kg for job 3. How much is left?

Answer:

QUESTION 9

An auto electrician has a 2 m length of ignition coil. If 35 cm is used on one job, 76 cm on another and 44 cm on the last job, how much is left?

Answer:

QUESTION 10

A set of speakers needs to be re-wired. If the mechanic has 6 m of wire and uses 257 cm, how much is left?

Answer:

Section C: Multiplication

Short-answer questions

Specific instructions to students

- This section will help you to improve your multiplication skills when working with decimals.
- Read the following questions and answer all of them in the spaces provided.
- You may not use a calculator.
- You need to show all of your working out.

QUESTION 1

If one tyre costs £99.95 and a mechanic replaces all five tyres in a car (including the spare tyre), how much will the total cost be?

Answer:

QUESTION 2

If a paint sprayer uses 16 litres of paint and, 1 litre costs £10.50, what is the total?

Answer:

QUESTION 3

A mechanic replaces six spark plugs at a cost of £4.50 each and four litres of oil at £3.99 per litre, what is the total cost?

Answer:

QUESTION 4

If a panel beater uses six packets of 12 mm nuts that cost £8.65 each, how much is the total cost?

Answer:

QUESTION 5

An auto electrician buys 12 packets of fuses that cost £9.95 each. What is the total cost?

Answer:

QUESTION 6

A mechanic earns £33.50 per hour. If the working week totals 45 hours, how much is earned?

Answer:

QUESTION 7

A workshop buys air conditioning hose for £2.55 per metre. If they purchase 25 metres, how much did they spend?

Answer:

_____

QUESTION 8

A car driver fills up her 52-litre tank with diesel at £1.85 per litre. How much does the driver pay?

Answer:

_____

QUESTION 9

A petrol station manager purchases 3400 litres of petrol for £1.15 per litre. What is the outlay?

Answer:

_____

QUESTION 10

A panel beater earns £180.65 per day. How much is earned for a 5-day week?

Answer:

_____

Section D: Division

Short-answer questions

Specific instructions to students

- This section will help you to improve your division skills when working with decimals.
- Read the following questions and answer all of them in the spaces provided.
- You may not use a calculator.
- You need to show all of your working out.

QUESTION 1

A paint sprayer has 28.5 litres of paint that is to be used on six separate jobs. How much needs to be allocated for each job?

Answer:

_____

QUESTION 2

A mechanic earns £990.60 for 5 days of work. How much is earned per day?

Answer:

_____

QUESTION 3

A taxi takes a fare and the final total is £32.70. If the taxi travels 25 miles, how much is the fare per mile?

Answer:

_____

QUESTION 4

An auto electrician completes a job worth £440.85. If the job took 16 hours, how much is it worth per hour?

Answer:

_____

QUESTION 5

A delivery driver drives from Penzance to Inverness and completes 720 miles in 3 days. How far has been travelled, on average, each day?

Answer:

_____

QUESTION 6

A parts supplier drives from London to Inverness travelling 562 miles. Nine hours has been spent driving. How far has been travelled for each hour of driving?

Answer:

_____

QUESTION 7

A car uses 36 litres to travel 575.8 miles. How far does the car travel per litre?

Answer:

QUESTION 8

A workshop buys 360 spark plugs in bulk at a total cost of £2290. How much is the cost of one spark plug?

Answer:

QUESTION 9

It costs £98.95 to fill a 52-litre fuel tank. How much is the cost per litre?

Answer:

QUESTION 10

A 50 m roll of heater hose costs £83.60. How much does it cost per metre?

Answer:

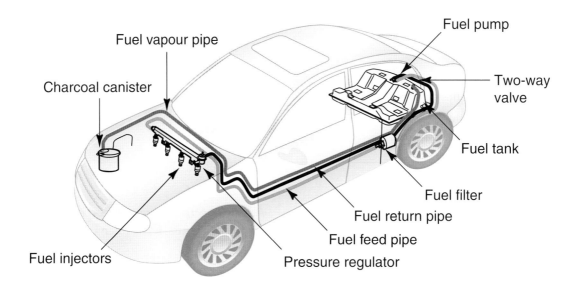

Fuel pump

Fuel vapour pipe

Two-way valve

Charcoal canister

Fuel tank

Fuel filter

Fuel return pipe

Fuel feed pipe

Fuel injectors

Pressure regulator

Section E: Valve clearance shims

You are rebuilding the cylinder head on an overhead cam engine. When you measured the valve clearances and shims, you wrote down the following values for cylinder number one:

Inlet valve clearance = 0.25mm   Inlet shim = 2.36mm

Exhaust valve clearance = 0.37mm   Exhaust shim = 2.38mm

If the manufacturer's specifications show a tolerance of 0.18mm to 0.23mm for the inlet and 0.28mm to 0.33mm for the exhaust, what size of shim would you select for the inlet and the exhaust?

Answer:

Unit 12: Fractions

Section A: Addition

Short-answer questions

Specific instructions to students

- This section is designed to help you to improve your addition skills when working with fractions.
- Read the following questions and answer all of them in the spaces provided.
- You may not use a calculator.
- You need to show all of your working out.

QUESTION 1

$\frac{1}{2} + \frac{4}{5} =$

Answer:

QUESTION 2

$\frac{22}{4} + \frac{12}{3} =$

Answer:

QUESTION 3

A mechanic pours $\frac{1}{3}$ of a bottle of brake fluid into a container. Another $\frac{1}{4}$ is added from another bottle. How much in total is there as a fraction?

Answer:

QUESTION 4

One can of axle grease has $\frac{1}{3}$ in it. Another can has $\frac{2}{5}$. How much axle grease is there in total, as a fraction?

Answer:

QUESTION 5

A paint sprayer has $1\frac{4}{5}$ cans of automotive red paint. To make a shade of orange another $1\frac{1}{6}$ cans of automotive yellow paint is added. How much paint is there in total, as a fraction?

Answer:

Section B: Subtraction

Short-answer questions

Specific instructions to students

- This section is designed to help you to improve your subtraction skills when working with fractions.
- Read the following questions and answer all of them in the spaces provided.
- You may not use a calculator.
- You need to show all of your working out.

QUESTION 1

$\frac{2}{3} - \frac{1}{4} =$

Answer:

QUESTION 2

$2\frac{2}{3} - 1\frac{1}{4} =$

Answer:

QUESTION 3

A crash repairer starts a repair job with $\frac{2}{3}$ of a can of filler. If a further $\frac{1}{3}$ is used on the job, how much filler is left as a fraction?

Answer:

QUESTION 4

A mechanic has $2\frac{1}{2}$ containers of transmission fluid. If $1\frac{1}{3}$ is used on two cars, how much transmission oil is left as a fraction?

Answer:

QUESTION 5

An apprentice has $2\frac{3}{4}$ containers of coolant to top up radiators on several cars in a workshop. If $1\frac{1}{2}$ is used to top up a radiator on the first car, how much is left in total as a fraction?

Answer:

Section C: Multiplication

Short-answer questions

Specific instructions to students

- This section is designed to help you to improve your multiplication skills when working with fractions.
- Read the following questions and answer all of them in the spaces provided.
- You may not use a calculator.
- You need to show all of your working out.

QUESTION 1

$\frac{2}{4} \times \frac{2}{3} =$

Answer:

QUESTION 2

$2\frac{2}{3} \times 1\frac{1}{2} =$

Answer:

QUESTION 3

A mechanic cuts two lengths of radiator hose that measure $18\frac{1}{2}$ cm each. What is the total length cut?

Answer:

QUESTION 4

A car needs three lengths of air conditioning hose that each measure $15\frac{1}{2}$ cm.

How much air conditioning hose is needed in total?

Answer:

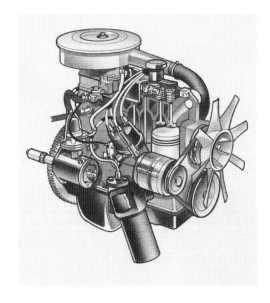

QUESTION 5

A battery requires four lengths of $10\frac{1}{2}$ cm steel to lock it into position. How much steel is needed in total?

Answer:

Section D: Division

Short-answer questions

Specific instructions to students

- This section is designed to help you to improve your division skills when working with fractions.
- Read the following questions and answer all of them in the spaces provided.
- You may not use a calculator.
- You need to show all of your working out.

QUESTION 1

$\frac{2}{3} \div \frac{1}{4} =$

Answer:

QUESTION 2

$2\frac{3}{4} \div 1\frac{1}{3} =$

Answer:

QUESTION 3

An apprentice has a length of radiator hose that measures $26\frac{1}{2}$ cm, and two equal lengths of radiator hose need to be cut. How long is each piece?

Answer:

QUESTION 4

A crash repairer has $1\frac{2}{3}$ cans of paint. If the paint is used on three separate jobs, how much as a fraction will be used on each job?

Answer:

QUESTION 5

A paint sprayer has $2\frac{2}{3}$ cans of automotive paint that is used on two jobs. How much as a fraction is used on each job?

Answer:

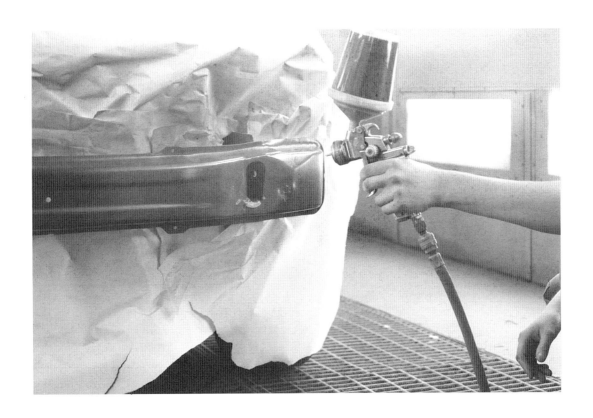

Unit 13: Percentages

Short-answer questions

Specific instructions to students

- In this unit, you will be able to practise and improve your skills in working out percentages.
- Read the following questions and answer all of them in the spaces provided.
- You may not use a calculator.
- You need to show all of your working out.

> **10% rule: Move the decimal one place to the left to get 10%.**

EXAMPLE

10% of £45.00 would be £4.50

QUESTION 1

If a vehicle repair bill comes to £220.00, how much is 10% of the bill?

Answer:

QUESTION 2

If a wireless reversing camera costs £249.00, what is 10% of the cost?

Answer:

QUESTION 3

A workshop buys a 2 hp direct drive air compressor for £198.50. If they were given a 10% discount, how much would the air compressor cost? (Find 10% and subtract it from the cost of the air compressor.)

Answer:

QUESTION 4

A mechanic buys 5 litres of oil for £14.80. A 5% discount is given. How much does the oil cost after the discount? (Hint: find 10%, halve it, then subtract it from £14.80.)

Answer:

QUESTION 5

A trade's assistant buys three roller storage bins for £20, a 12 V air compressor for £69 and a pair of car seat covers for £169. How much is the total? And how much is it after a 10% discount?

Answer:

QUESTION 6

The following items are purchased for a workshop: a fluorescent work light for £39.99, a crimping tool kit for £9.99, an air horn for £19.99, a digital multimeter for £12.99, a set of vehicle rear tail lights for £49.99 and a 25 m length of cable for £14.99. What is the total? And what is the final cost after a 10% discount?

Answer:

QUESTION 7

An automotive store offers 20% off the price of sets of spark plugs. If a set is priced at £36 before the discount, how much will they cost after the discount?

Answer:

QUESTION 8

Fan belts are discounted by 15%. If the regular retail price is £15.50 each, what is the discounted price?

Answer:

QUESTION 9

A set of alloy wheel lock nuts costs £16.90 at the regular retail price. If the store has a 20% sale, how much will they cost during the sale?

Answer:

QUESTION 10

A 1200 Amp (A) starting booster pack retails for £99. How much will it cost after the store takes off 30%?

Answer:

Unit 14: Measurement Conversions

Short-answer questions

Specific instructions to students

- This unit is designed to help you to both improve your conversion skills and to increase your speed in converting one measurement unit into another.
- Read the following questions and answer all of them in the spaces provided.
- You may not use a calculator.
- You need to show all of your working out.

QUESTION 1

How many millimetres are there in 1 centimetre?

Answer:

QUESTION 2

How many millimetres are there in 1 metre?

Answer:

QUESTION 3

How many centimetres are there in 1 metre?

Answer:

QUESTION 4

If a screw has 20 threads in 2 centimetres, how many threads would there be in 10 centimetres?

Answer:

QUESTION 5

How many ml are there in 4.8 litres of engine oil?

Answer:

QUESTION 6

3500 ml of coolant makes up how many litres?

Answer:

QUESTION 7

A small car body weighs $\frac{1}{2}$ a tonne. How many kg is that?

Answer:

QUESTION 8

A pickup truck weighs 2 tonnes. How much does it weigh in kg?

Answer:

QUESTION 9

A truck weighs 4750 kgs. How many tonnes is that?

Answer:

QUESTION 10

A trailer measures 180 cm in length and 120 cm across the back. How far is it around the perimeter of the trailer?

Answer:

Section A: Circumference

Short-answer questions

Specific instructions to students

- This section is designed to help you to both improve your measuring skills and to increase your speed in measuring the circumference of a round object.
- Read the following questions and answer all of them in the spaces provided.
- You may not use a calculator.
- You will to show all of your working out.

$C = \pi \times d$

where:

C = circumference

$\pi = 3.14$

d = diameter

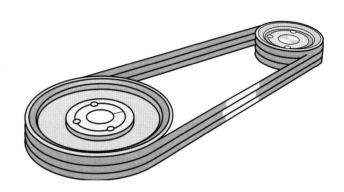

EXAMPLE

Find the circumference of a wheel with a diameter of 30 cm.

$C = \pi \times d$

Therefore, $C = 3.14 \times 30$

$\qquad = 94.2$ cm

QUESTION 1

Find the circumference of a wheel with a diameter of 200 cm.

Answer:

QUESTION 2

Calculate the circumference of a pulley with a diameter of 15 cm.

Answer:

QUESTION 3

Find the circumference of a headlight with a diameter of 32 cm.

Answer:

QUESTION 4

Determine the circumference of the head of an inlet valve with a diameter of 5 cm.

Answer:

QUESTION 5

Calculate the circumference of a distributor cap with a diameter of 30 cm.

Answer:

QUESTION 6

Find the circumference of a front brake disc with a diameter of 28.8 cm.

Answer:

QUESTION 7

Determine the circumference of a speaker with a diameter of 45.6 cm.

Answer:

_____

QUESTION 8

Find the circumference of a 1200 watt (W) sander with a diameter of 14.3 cm.

Answer:

_____

QUESTION 9

Calculate the circumference of a brake drum with a diameter of 42.9 cm.

Answer:

_____

QUESTION 10

Find the circumference of a 500 W sub woofer with a diameter of 18.8 cm.

Answer:

_____

Section B: Diameter

Short-answer questions

Specific instructions to students

- This section is designed to help you to both improve your measuring skills and to increase your speed in measuring the diameter of a round object.
- Read the following questions and answer all of them in the spaces provided.
- You may not use a calculator.
- You need to show all of your working out.

$$\text{Diameter } (d) \text{ of a circle} = \frac{\text{circumference}}{\pi(3.14)}$$

EXAMPLE

Find the diameter of a brake disc with a circumference of 110 cm.

$$d = \frac{110}{3.14}$$
$$= 35.03 \text{ cm}$$

QUESTION 1

Find the diameter of a steering wheel with a circumference of 120 cm.

Answer:

_____

QUESTION 2

Calculate the diameter of an exhaust silencer with a circumference of 16 cm.

Answer:

_____

QUESTION 3

Find the diameter of a lamp unit with a circumference of 20 cm.

Answer:

_____

QUESTION 4

Determine the diameter of a 600 W sub woofer with a circumference of 130 cm.

Answer:

_____

QUESTION 5

Calculate the diameter of a tyre with a circumference of 210 cm.

Answer:

_____

QUESTION 6

Find the diameter of an alloy wheel lock nut with a circumference of 11.8 cm.

Answer:

_____

QUESTION 7

Calculate the diameter of a radiator hose with a circumference of 12.4 cm.

Answer:

QUESTION 8

Find the diameter of a brake disc with a circumference of 90.8 cm.

Answer:

QUESTION 9

Determine the diameter of an air filter with a circumference of 100 cm.

Answer:

QUESTION 10

Find the diameter of an oil filter with a circumference of 32.8 cm.

Answer:

Section C: Area

Short-answer questions

Specific instructions to students

- This section is designed to help you to both improve your measuring skills and to increase your speed in measuring surface area.
- Read the following questions and answer all of them in the spaces provided.
- You may not use a calculator.
- You need to show all of your working out.

> **Area = length × width and is given in square units.**
> $$= l \times w$$

QUESTION 1

The length of the inside of a box trailer is 30 m by 2.8 m wide, what is the total area?

Answer:

QUESTION 2

If a workshop measures 60 m by 13 m, what is the total area?

Answer:

QUESTION 3

A sheet of fibreglass is 2.85 m by 1.65 m. What is the total area?

Answer:

QUESTION 4

If a car hoist is 4.5 m by 1.8 m, what is the total area?

Answer:

QUESTION 5

Gasket material can be purchased by the square metre. What is the total area of a 30 m roll that is 1.50 m wide?

Answer:

QUESTION 6

If a battery has plates inside of it that measure 15.5 cm by 12.8 cm, what is the total area of one plate?

Answer:

QUESTION 7

The boot of a sports tourer is 1.06 m by 1.07 m. What is the total boot floor area?

Answer:

QUESTION 8

A vehicle sales area is 65.3 m by 32.7 m. How much floor area is there?

Answer:

QUESTION 9

If a carport is 3.2 m wide by 8.6 m long, what is its floor area?

Answer:

QUESTION 10

A removal van is 8.9 m long and 2.6 m wide. How much floor area is there?

Answer:

Section D: Volume of a cube

Short-answer questions

Specific instructions to students

- This section is designed to help you to both improve your measuring skills and to increase your speed in calculating volumes of rectangular or square objects.
- Read the following questions and answer all of them in the spaces provided.
- You may not use a calculator.
- You need to show all of your working out.

> **Volume = length × width × height and is given in cubic units.**
> $$= l \times w \times h$$

QUESTION 1

How many cubic metres are there in a storage area 13 m by 5 m by 4 m?

Answer:

QUESTION 2

If a recovery truck has the dimensions of 8 m by 3 m by 4 m, how many cubic metres are available?

Answer:

QUESTION 3

A box trailer used for transporting drag racing cars is 38 m long by 3 m high by 6 m wide. How many cubic metres are there?

Answer:

_____

QUESTION 4

If a welder constructs a small trailer 2.2 m by 1.8 m by 0.5 m, how many cubic metres are available?

Answer:

_____

QUESTION 5

A mechanic's assistant makes a new tool box with the following dimensions: 600 mm by 150 mm by 100 mm. How many cubic millimetres have been made?

Answer:

_____

QUESTION 6

A MIG welder stands 1.2 m × 0.6 m × 0.5 m. What cubic area does it take up?

Answer:

_____

QUESTION 7

A spare parts box is 1 m long, 60 cm wide and 75 cm tall. How many cubic centimetres are available for storing parts?

Answer:

_____

QUESTION 8

The boot of a people carrier is 1.4 m wide × 1.6 m long × 88 cm high. What is its cubic area in centimetres?

Answer:

_____

QUESTION 9

A panel beater works on a panel van that is 1.75 m high by 1.35 m wide by 3.6 m long. What is its total volume in cubic metres?

Answer:

_____

QUESTION 10

A paint sprayer needs to spray a room 3.8 m × 3.8 m × 2.5 m. How many cubic metres does he need to cover?

Answer:

_____

Section E: Volume of a cylinder

Short-answer questions

Specific instructions to students

- This section is designed to help you to both improve your measuring skills and to increase your speed in calculating volumes of cylindrical objects.
- Read the following questions and answer all of them in the spaces provided.
- You may not use a calculator.
- You need to show all of your working out.

Volume of a cylinder $(V_c) = \pi\,(3.14) \times r^2$
(radius × radius) ×
height

$$V_c = \pi \times r^2 \times h$$

QUESTION 1

What is the volume of a drum that has a radius of 10 cm and a height of 50 cm ?

Answer:

_____

QUESTION 2

What is the volume of a can of degreaser that has a radius of 3 cm and a height of 20 cm?

Answer:

_____

QUESTION 3

A canister of axle grease has a radius of 4 cm and a height of 11 cm. What is its volume?

Answer:

_____

QUESTION 4

An oil can has a radius of 5 cm and a length of 28 cm. How much grease can it hold?

Answer:

___

QUESTION 5

A can of lock oil has a radius of 5 cm and a height of 16.5 cm. What is its volume?

Answer:

___

QUESTION 6

A mechanic has a can of degreaser that has a radius of 3 cm and a height of 25 cm. What is its volume?

Answer:

___

QUESTION 7

A 5 l container of anti-freeze gets poured into three containers. Each container has a radius of 5 cm and a height of 20 cm.

a What is the volume of each container?

Answer:

___

b What is the volume of all three containers in total?

Answer:

___

c How much is left in the 5 litre container?

Answer:

___

QUESTION 8

A container of body filler has a radius of 10 cm and a height of 15 cm.

a What is its volume?

Answer:

___

b If you use half on one job, how much is left?

Answer:

___

QUESTION 9

A can of general purpose thinners has a radius of 11 cm and a height of 22 cm.

a What is its volume?

Answer:

___

b If you use 750 cm³, how much is left?

Answer:

___

QUESTION 10

A panel beater uses a can of body filler that has a radius of 6 cm and a height of 18 cm. What is its volume?

Answer:

___

Unit 16: Earning Wages

Short-answer questions

Specific instructions to students

- This unit will help you to calculate how much a job is worth and how much time you will need to complete the job.
- Read the following questions and answer all of them in the spaces provided.
- You may not use a calculator.
- You need to show all of your working out.

QUESTION 1

A first-year automotive apprentice earns £260.60 net (take home) per week. How much does he earn per year?

Answer:

_____

QUESTION 2

A panel beater starts work at 8.00 a.m. and stops for a break at 10.30 a.m. for 20 minutes. Lunch starts at 12 noon and finishes at 1.00 p.m. and he then works through to 4.00 p.m. How many hours have been worked?

Answer:

_____

QUESTION 3

A mechanic's assistant earns £15.50 an hour and works a 38-hour week. How much is his gross earnings (before tax)?

Answer:

_____

QUESTION 4

Over a week, a paint sprayer completes five jobs which cost as follows: £465.80; £2490.50; £556.20; £1560.70 and £990.60. What is the total?

Answer:

_____

QUESTION 5

A panel beater needs to remove a front panel that takes 34 minutes; a bumper which takes 18 minutes; two headlights that takes 7 minutes; the bonnet which takes 14 minutes and a door that takes 9 minutes. How much time will be needed for this job? State the answer in hours and minutes.

Answer:

_____

QUESTION 6

The front end of a car needs to be removed before it can be rebuilt. This takes the panel beater $4\frac{1}{2}$ hours. If the hourly rate is £28.60, how much will the total be?

Answer:

_____

QUESTION 7

A major service takes $1\frac{1}{2}$ hours to complete. If the mechanic is getting paid £34.80 per hour, what is the total?

Answer:

_____

QUESTION 8

A car that has hit a tree has major damage. The workshop team spent 56 hours working on it. If they worked 8 hours per day, how many days did it take to repair?

Answer:

_____

QUESTION 9

A mechanic begins work at 7 a.m. and works until 4 p.m. There is a morning break for 20 minutes, a lunch break for 60 minutes and an afternoon break for 20 minutes.

a How much time has been spent on breaks?

Answer:

_____

b How much time has been spent working?

Answer:

_____

QUESTION 10

A crash repair job costs £2850.50 to complete (including parts and labour). The repairer spends 12 hours on the job. How much is the rate per hour?

Answer:

_____

QUESTION 11

The total cost of replacing front and rear brake linings comes to £375.50. If it took two mechanics 3 hours to complete and clean up afterwards, how much is the cost per hour?

Answer:

_____

QUESTION 12

An apprentice technician starts work at 7.30 a.m. ordering parts and checking stock and works until 3.30 p.m. She had a morning break for 20 minutes, a lunch break for 60 minutes and an afternoon break of 20 minutes.

a How much time has she spent on breaks?

Answer:

_____

b How much time has been spent working?

Answer:

_____

QUESTION 13

The total cost of a full car service and MOT comes to £237.50. If it took the two mechanics 5 hours to complete and clean up afterwards, how much is the cost per hour?

Answer:

_____

QUESTION 14

Fill in the gaps on the timesheet, using the instructions and information below.

James works a 5-hour shift.

Alan works for 4.5 hours.

Emma works for 6 hours and 45 minutes and gets paid £2.50 less than Alan.

Tim earns £1.75 more per hour than James and works for 7.5 hours with a half hour unpaid break in the middle of his shift.

Name	Time in	Time out	Rate of pay	Total
James	10:00		£6.50	
Alan		12:30	£10.45	£47.03
Adam	7:45		£7.50	£33.75
Emma		16:00		
Tim	13:50			

Unit 17: Squaring Numbers

Section A: Introducing square numbers

Short-answer questions

Specific instructions to students

- This section is designed to help you to both improve your skills and to increase your speed in squaring numbers.
- Read the following questions and answer all of them in the spaces provided.
- You may not use a calculator.
- You need to show all of your working out.

> **Any number squared is multiplied by itself.**

EXAMPLE

4 squared $= 4^2 = 4 \times 4 = 16$

QUESTION 1

$6^2 =$

Answer:

_____

QUESTION 2

$8^2 =$

Answer:

_____

QUESTION 3

$12^2 =$

Answer:

_____

QUESTION 4

$3^2 =$

Answer:

_____

QUESTION 5

$7^2 =$

Answer:

_____

QUESTION 6

$11^2 =$

Answer:

_____

QUESTION 7

$10^2 =$

Answer:

_____

QUESTION 8

$9^2 =$

Answer:

_____

QUESTION 9

$2^2 =$

Answer:

_____

QUESTION 10

$4^2 =$

Answer:

_____

QUESTION 11

$5^2 =$

Answer:

_____

Section B: Applying square numbers to the trade

Worded practical problems

Specific instructions to students

- This section is designed to help you to both improve your skills and to increase your speed in calculating volumes of rectangular or square objects.
- Read the following questions and answer all of them in the spaces provided.
- You may not use a calculator.
- You need to show all of your working out.

QUESTION 1

A paint sprayer needs to spray an area which measures 2.8×2.8 metres. What area does it take up?

Answer:

QUESTION 2

A workshop has a welding area that is 5.2×5.2 metres. What is the total area?

Answer:

QUESTION 3

The dimensions of a garage are 12.6×12.6 metres. What is the total area?

Answer:

QUESTION 4

A mechanic works in an area that is 15×15 metres.

If there is an area allocated for storage which is 2.4×2.4 metres, how much area is left for the mechanic to work in?

Answer:

QUESTION 5

An auto electrician has a total work area of 13.8×13.8 metres. The spare parts area takes up 1.2×1.2 metres and the tool area is 2.7×2.7 metres. How much area is left to work in?

Answer:

QUESTION 6

A panel beater has a sheet of metal 2.4 × 2.4 metres. If 1.65 × 1.65 metres is cut out of it, how much is left?

Answer:

QUESTION 7

A welder cuts out a square piece of metal of 50 × 50 cm from a sheet that measures 1.2 × 1.2 metres. How much is left?

Answer:

QUESTION 8

A concrete work floor measures 28.2 × 28.2 metres. If it costs £9.50 to paint 1 square metre, how much will it cost to paint the whole floor?

Answer:

QUESTION 9

Four walls of a warehouse need to be insulated. The total wall area measures 200 × 200 metres. If it costs £6.80 to insulate one square metre, how much will it cost to insulate the whole wall area of the workshop?

Answer:

QUESTION 10

The four walls of a welding area measure 2.6 × 2.6 metres each. To insulate 1 square metre it costs £28.50. How much will it cost to insulate all four walls?

Answer:

Section A: Introducing ratios

Short-answer questions

Specific instructions to students

- This section is designed to help you improve your skills in calculating and simplifying ratios.
- Read the following questions and answer all of them in the spaces provided.
- You may not use a calculator.
- You need to show all of your working out.
- Reduce the ratios to the simplest or lowest form.

QUESTION 1

The number of teeth on Gear 1 is 40. The number of teeth on Gear 2 is 20. What is the ratio of Gear 1 to Gear 2?

Answer:

QUESTION 2

Pulley A has a diameter of 60 cm and Pulley B has a diameter of 15 cm. What is the ratio of diameters A to B?

Answer:

QUESTION 3

Pulley A has a diameter of 48 cm and Pulley B has a diameter of 16 cm. What is the ratio of diameters A to B?

Answer:

QUESTION 4

Two gears have 75 and 15 teeth respectively. What is the ratio?

Answer:

QUESTION 5

Three gears have 80 : 60 : 20 teeth respectively. What is the ratio?

Answer:

QUESTION 6

One car wheel has a diameter of 38 cm and a truck wheel has a diameter of 60 cm. What is the ratio?

Answer:

QUESTION 7

The diameter of an air filter is 32 cm, an oil filter is 16 cm and another filter is 48 cm. What is the ratio?

Answer:

QUESTION 8

Three wheel diameters from a sport tourer, a minibus and an HGV are: 38 cm, 76 cm and 114 cm respectively. What is the ratio?

Answer:

QUESTION 9

Pulley A has a diameter of 34 cm and Pulley B has a diameter of 12 cm. What is the ratio?

Answer:

QUESTION 10

The circumference of Pulley A is 62 cm and the circumference of Pulley B is 38 cm. What is the ratio?

Answer:

Section B: Applying ratios to the trade

Short-answer questions

Specific instructions to students

- This section is designed to help you improve your practical skills when working with ratios.
- Read the following questions and answer all of them in the spaces provided.
- You may not use a calculator.
- You need to show all of your working out.

QUESTION 1

The ratio of the teeth on gear 1 to gear 2 is 3 : 1. If gear 2 has 10 teeth, how many teeth will gear 1 have?

Answer:

QUESTION 2

The ratio of the teeth on gear 1 to gear 2 is 2 : 1. If gear 2 has 20 teeth, how many teeth will gear 1 have?

Answer:

QUESTION 3

The ratio of the diameters of pulley A to pulley B is 40 : 20. What is the lowest ratio of the diameter of pulley A to pulley B?

Answer:

QUESTION 4

The ratio of the diameters of pulley A to pulley B is 20 : 10. What is the lowest ratio of the diameter of pulley A to pulley B?

Answer:

QUESTION 5

The ratio of diameters of gear A to gear B is 3 : 1. If the diameter of gear A is 12 cm, what is the diameter of gear B?

Answer:

QUESTION 6

The ratio of diameters of gear A to gear B is 2 : 1. If the diameter of gear A is 17 cm, what is the diameter of gear B?

Answer:

QUESTION 7

The ratio of diameters of gear A to gear B is 3 : 1. If the diameter of gear A is 21 cm, what is the diameter of gear B?

Answer:

QUESTION 8

The ratio of diameters of gear A to gear B is 3 : 2. If the diameter of gear A is 9 cm, what is the diameter of gear B?

Answer:

QUESTION 9

The ratio of diameters of gear A to gear B is 4 : 3. If the diameter of gear A is 16 cm, what is the diameter of gear B?

Answer:

QUESTION 10

The ratio of diameters of gear A to gear B is 4 : 3. If the diameter of gear A is 24 cm, what is the diameter of gear B?

Answer:

Unit 19: Mechanical Reasoning

Short-answer questions

Specific instructions to students

- This section is designed to help you improve your skills in mechanical reasoning.
- Read the following questions and answer all of them in the spaces provided.
- You may not use a calculator.
- You need to show all of your working out.
- Reduce the ratios to the simplest or lowest form.

QUESTION 1

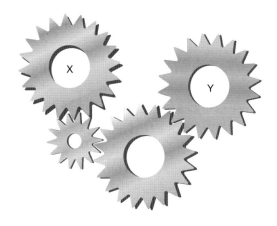

If gear X turns in a clockwise direction, which way will gear Y turn?

Answer:

QUESTION 2

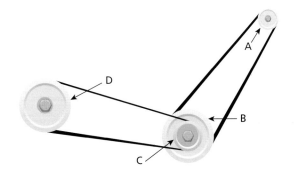

If pulley A turns in a clockwise direction, which way will pulley D turn?

Answer:

QUESTION 3

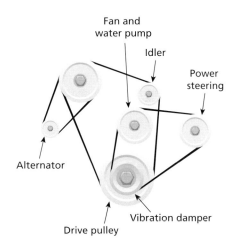

If the drive pulley in a work van engine turns in a clockwise direction, in which direction will the alternator turn?

Answer:

QUESTION 4

Looking at the following diagram, if lever A moves to the left, in which direction will lever B move?

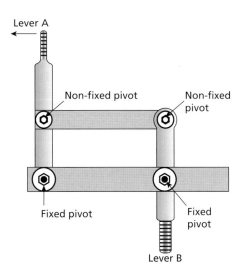

Answer:

QUESTION 5

In the following diagram, pulley 1 turns clockwise. In what direction will pulley 6 turn?

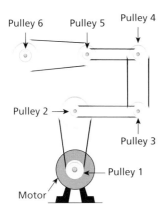

Answer:

_____

QUESTION 6

If lever A is pulled up, what will happen to lever B?

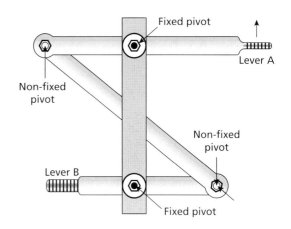

Answer:

_____

Unit 20: Reading, Interpreting and Understanding Information In Tables, Charts and Graphs

Section A: Information displayed in tables

Information is often displayed in tables and charts for people to read to retrieve various bits of information. This is common in day-to-day activities such as timetables for buses and trains, viewing sales figures for different products or the results of a questionnaire.

In the automotive industry, tables are often used to record test results or to compare performance data of vehicle components, materials and machines. Have a look at the table below, relating to accidents reported to the Health and Safety Executive, and answer the questions that follow.

The table shows typical stopping distances included in the Highway code.

Speed (mph)	20	30	40	50	60	70	80
Thinking distance (m)	6	9	12	15	18	21	24
Braking distance (m)	6	14	24	38	54	75	96
Total stopping distance (m)	12	23	36	53	72	96	120

QUESTION 1

How many categories of speeds are shown in the table?

Answer:

QUESTION 2

How is the total stopping distance calculated?

Answer:

QUESTION 3

Describe the relationship between the speed and the total stopping distance?

Answer:

QUESTION 4

By how much does the total stopping distance increase between 20mph and 80mph? Record your answer as a percentage.

Answer:

Section B: Information displayed in charts

Similar to the use of tables, charts provide a graphical and simplified view of what can sometimes represent a large amount of information, or data.

Using the data from the stopping distances table in Section A, draw a column chart to compare the relationship between the speed (mph) and the total stopping distance (m) using the grid below.

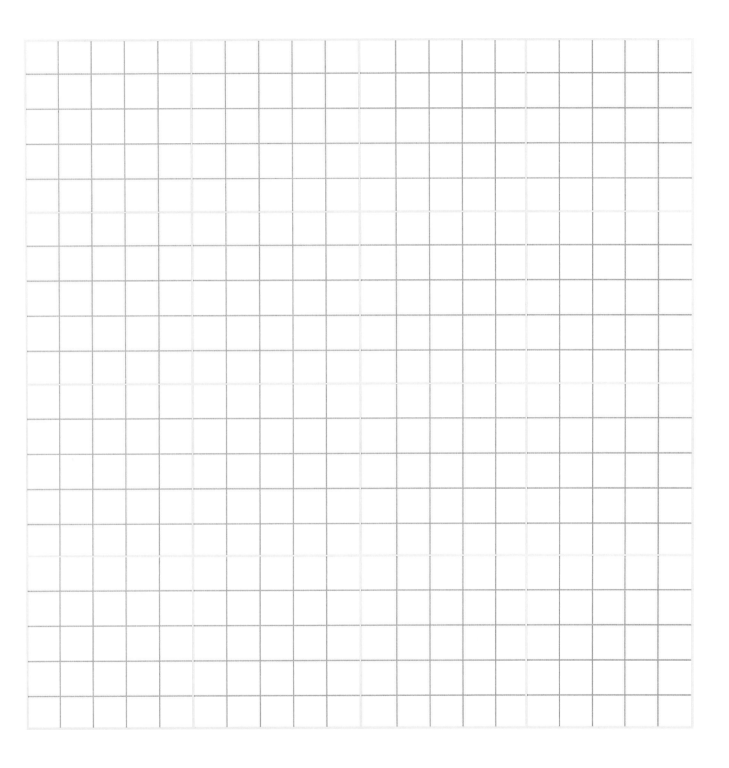

Unit 21: Vehicle Modification Costs

Use the vehicle modification activity from Unit 6 Section B that you carried out and answer the following:

QUESTION 1

Create a spreadsheet to show all of the new parts and any materials that you would need, then add a column with the full cost of each item.

Use http://www.eurocarparts.com/ to help you find accurate costs for your parts and materials.

QUESTION 2

What is the total cost of your modifications?

QUESTION 3

If the total budget for your modifications was £4500, are you over budget or under budget.

QUESTION 4

If the motor factory is prepared to give you a discount of 9% on parts and 12% on materials, what will the final cost of parts and materials be?

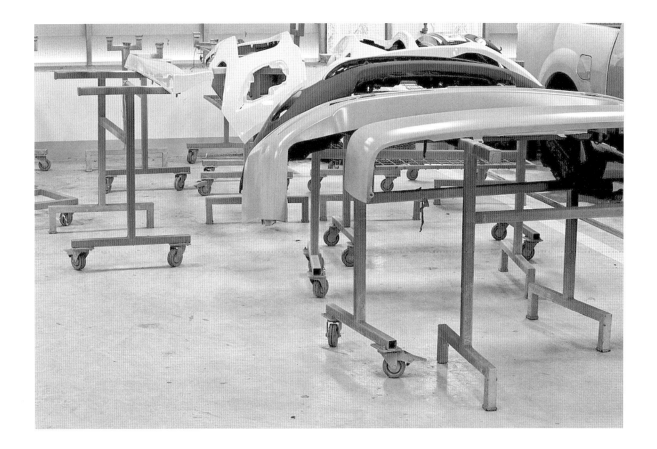

Unit 22:
Practice Written Exam for the Automotive Trade

Reading time: 10 minutes

Writing time: 1 hour 30 minutes

Section A: Literacy

Section B: General Mathematics

Section C: Trade Mathematics

QUESTION and ANSWER BOOK

Section	Topic	Number of questions	Marks
A B C	Literacy General Mathematics Trade Mathematics	7 11 42 Total 60	22 24 54 Total 100

The sections may be completed in the order of your choice.

NO CALCULATORS are to be used during the exam.

Spelling

Read the passage below, then underline the 20 spelling errors.

10 marks

A garuge has 18 cars in for servises. Six of the cars also need body work due to minor collitions that had happened during the recent wet weather. The apprentice had to go to the storerom to retreve the spark plugs that were needed to repair some of the other cars. Meenwhile, the other two mechanics began work on the Ford Focus. The windskreen needed to be replased as it had a mojor crack through it from the lower ritte side up through the left side. The vehicle driver had been following a lorry when it kicked up a stone and hit directly on the windscreen. The driver swurved as the stone hit the car and ended up hitting a telegraf pole, then ended up in a ditch. This caused damige along the driver's side front wheel and panel. Major panell beating and respraying had to be undartaken to bring the car back to its original condision.

In addision, the steering needed checking, the radiater needed a complete re-build and the alternater was damaged beyond repair and needed replacing. The head mekanic wanted the work completed by the end of the day so that there was no work to be done over the weekend.

Correct the spelling errors by writing them out with the correct spelling below.

_____

_____

Alphabetizing

Put the following words into alphabetical order.

6 marks

Wheel alignment	Gearbox
Tail light	Air horn
Spark plugs	Electronic ignition
Rear end	Seat belt
Exhaust pipe	Provisional license
Inlet valves	LPG (Liquid Petroleum Gas)

_____

_____

_____

_____

_____

_____

Comprehension

Short-answer questions

Specific instructions to students

- Read the following activity and then answer the questions accordingly.

Read the following passage and then answer the questions below.

It was 5 o'clock in the morning when three mates got up to go fishing. Clinton had a Renault Megane Scenic that fitted all of their fishing gear, so they took his car. Clinton picked up Daniel and Matthew before heading for the petrol station. As they pulled into the service station, Clinton realized that he needed to check the oil, fill up with petrol and top up the automatic transmission fluid. All hadn't been checked for a while and it was an hour and a half down the road to their favourite fishing lake.

Daniel started filling the petrol tank. It was on empty. The price of unleaded petrol was £1.58 per litre and he filled up with 51 litres. The car also had LPG, so they decided to fill that tank too. It took 33 litres at 68 pence per litre. Meanwhile, Clinton and Matthew checked the engine oil and found that it was down to $\frac{3}{8}$ full and so Matthew topped it up. The automatic transmission oil was $\frac{3}{4}$ full so Clinton didn't worry about adding any more.

After they had purchased some breakfast, they decided to check the tyre pressures. The two front tyres had 1.2 and 1.6 Bar in them. Both needed inflating to 2.2 Bar. The back two tyre pressures were not too bad and they didn't require more inflation. It was 6.15 a.m. when they finally left the service station for the fishing lake. The fishing was worth it. At around 2.45 p.m, they packed up as it started to rain and this made it very wet and cold. They arrived home tired and happy at 4.30 p.m.

QUESTION 1	1 mark

Why did they decide to take Clinton's car?

Answer:

_____

QUESTION 2	1 + 1 = 2 marks

How much did it cost to fill the car with:

a Petrol?

Answer:

_____

b LPG?

Answer:

_____

QUESTION 3   1 mark

How much engine oil was needed to top up the car?

Answer:

_____

QUESTION 4   1 mark

How much air was needed to inflate each of the front tyres?

Answer:

_____

QUESTION 5   1 mark

How far, in hours and minutes, were Clinton, Daniel and Matthew from home?

Answer:

_____

Section B: General Mathematics

QUESTION 1   1 + 1 + 1 = 3 marks

What unit of measurement would you use to measure:

a Amount of petrol?

Answer:

_____

b Engine temperature?

Answer:

_____

c Engine oil?

Answer:

_____

QUESTION 2   1 + 1 + 1 = 3 marks

For each of the following, give an example of where it may be found in the automotive industry:

a Percentages?

Answer:

_____

b Decimals?

Answer:

_____

c Fractions?

Answer:

_____

QUESTION 3   1 + 1 = 2 marks

Convert the following units:

a 3 kgs to grams

Answer:

_____

b 5 tonnes to kg

Answer:

_____

QUESTION 4   2 marks

Write the following in descending order:

0.7   0.71   7.1   70.1   701.00   7.0

Answer:

_____

QUESTION 5   1 + 1 = 2 marks

Write the decimal number that is between the following:

a 0.1 and 0.2

Answer:

_____

b 1.3 and 1.4

Answer:

_____

QUESTION 6   1 + 1 = 2 marks

Round off the following numbers to two (2) decimal places:

a 5.177

Answer:

_____

b 12.655

Answer:

___

QUESTION 7   1 + 1 = 2 marks
Estimate the following by approximation:

a 101×81

Answer:

___

b 399×21

Answer:

___

QUESTION 8   1 + 1 = 2 marks
What do the following add up to?

a £7, £13.57 and £163.99

Answer:

___

b 4, 5.73 and 229.57

Answer:

___

QUESTION 9   1 + 1 = 2 marks
Subtract the following:

a 196 from 813

Answer:

___

b 5556 from 9223

Answer:

___

QUESTION 10   1 + 1 = 2 marks
Use division to solve:

a $4824 \div 3$

Answer:

___

b $84.2 \div 0.4$

Answer:

___

QUESTION 11   1 + 1 = 2 marks
Using BODMAS solve:

a $(3 \times 7) \times 4 + 9 - 5 =$

Answer:

___

b $(8 \times 12) \times 2 + 8 - 4 =$

Answer:

___

Section C: Motor Trade Mathematics

Basic operations

Addition

QUESTION 1   1 mark
An auto electrician uses 6 m, 11 m, 23 m and 45 m of different types of electrical wire over 3 months. How much electrical wire has been used in total?

Answer:

___

QUESTION 2   1 mark
A mechanic charges £163 for labour for a service and £68 for parts. How much is the total bill?

Answer:

___

Subtraction

QUESTION 1   1 mark

A work van is filled up with 36 litres of diesel. The tank is now at its maximum of 52 litres. A driver uses the following amounts of diesel on each day:

Monday – 5 litres

Tuesday – 11 litres

Wednesday – 10 litres

Thursday – 8 litres

Friday – 7 litres

How many litres of diesel are left in the tank?

Answer:

QUESTION 2   1 mark

If a mechanic has 224 spark plugs in stock and 179 are used over 4 weeks in a garage, how many are left?

Answer:

Multiplication

QUESTION 1   1 mark

A crash repairer uses 24 nuts, 48 washers and 24 bolts on a car for particular work. How many nuts, washers and bolts would be used on 9 cars?

Answer:

QUESTION 2   1 mark

2 m of green wire, 3 m of red wire and 1m of yellow wire are used for connecting different electrical parts on one car. How much of each wire would be used doing the wiring on 12 cars?

Answer:

Division

QUESTION 1   1 mark

A mechanic has a box of 250 12 mm nuts. How many jobs can be completed if each standard job requires eight nuts? Are there any left over?

Answer:

QUESTION 2   1 mark

If an apprentice earns £288.80 for working a 5-day week, how much is earned per day?

Answer:

Decimals
Addition

QUESTION 1   1 mark

A set of speakers and a CD tuner are purchased for £217.99 and £256.50 respectively. How much will be paid in total?

Answer:

QUESTION 2   1 mark

An auto electrician buys a multimeter for £18.75, electrical tape for £6.95, a headlight bulb for £4.95 and a steering wheel cover for £17.50. How much has been spent?

Answer:

Subtraction

QUESTION 1   1 mark

A paint sprayer has a 4-litre can of paint. It is used on three different paint jobs: 1185 ml for job 1, 1560 ml on job 2 and 1135 ml on job 3. How much is left?

Answer:

QUESTION 2   1 mark

An auto electrician has a 6 m reel of cable. If 2.78 m is used on one job, 1.76 m on another and 1.44 m on the last job, how much is left on the reel?

Answer:

Multiplication

QUESTION 1   1 mark

A mechanic replaces six spark plugs at a cost of £6.99 each, and 4 litres of oil at £7.99 per litre. What is the total cost?

Answer:

QUESTION 2   1 mark

If a panel beater uses six packets of 12 mm nuts that cost £8.50 per packet, how much is the total cost?

Answer:

Division

QUESTION 1   1 mark

An auto electrician takes 12 hours to complete three jobs and the total bill is £582.48. How much is it per hour?

Answer:

QUESTION 2   1 mark

A workshop buys 240 spark plugs in bulk at a total cost of £1560. How much is the cost of one spark plug?

Answer:

Fractions

QUESTION 1   1 mark

$\frac{2}{3} + \frac{3}{4} =$

Answer:

QUESTION 2   1 mark

$\frac{4}{5} - \frac{1}{3} =$

Answer:

QUESTION 3   1 mark

$\frac{2}{3} \times \frac{1}{4} =$

Answer:

QUESTION 4   1 mark

$\frac{3}{4} \div \frac{1}{2} =$

Answer:

Percentages

QUESTION 1   1 + 1 = 2 marks

A crash repair bill comes to £1380.00.

a How much is 10% of the bill?

Answer:

b What is the final bill once 10% is taken off?

Answer:

QUESTION 2   1 + 1 = 2 marks

A person buys a new fan belt, a new alternator and a new water pump for their car. The total comes to £170.50.

a What is 10% of the total?

Answer:

b How much is the final total once the 10% is taken off?

Answer:

Measurement

QUESTION 1   1 mark

How many millilitres are there in 3.85 litres?

Answer:

_____

QUESTION 2   1 mark

2285 millilitres converts to how many litres?

Answer:

_____

Circumference

QUESTION 1   1 mark

What is the circumference of an alternator belt pulley
with a diameter of 14 cm?

Answer:

_____

QUESTION 2   1 mark

What is the circumference of a brake disc with a
diameter of 30 cm?

Answer:

_____

Diameter

QUESTION 1   1 mark

What is the diameter of a 600 W sub woofer with a
circumference of 140 cm?

Answer:

_____

QUESTION 2   1 mark

What is the diameter of a tyre with a circumference of
240 cm?

Answer:

_____

Area

QUESTION 1   1 mark

A trailer's base measures 2 m by 1.2 m; what is the total
area?

Answer:

_____

QUESTION 2   1 mark

A rectangular piece of gasket material measures 30 cm
long by 15 cm wide. What is its area?

Answer:

_____

Volume of a cube

QUESTION 1

                                                         2 marks

A small trailer measures 2 m $\times$ 2m $\times$ 0.5 m. How many
cubic metres is that?

Answer:

_____

QUESTION 2   2 marks

A new toolbox has the following dimensions: 60 cm by
15 cm by 10 cm. What is the total volume?

Answer:

_____

Volume of a cylinder

QUESTION 1   2 marks

A grease gun has a radius of 7 cm and a length of 30 cm.
How much grease can it hold?

Answer:

_____

QUESTION 2   2 marks

A container of body filler has a radius of 8 cm and a
height of 12 cm. What is its volume? If you use half on
one job, how much is left?

Answer:

_____

Earning wages

QUESTION 1   2 marks

A first year automotive apprentice earns £280.60 net (take home) per week. How much do they earn per year? Note that there are 52 weeks in a year.

Answer:

_____

QUESTION 2   2 marks

A car has major damage after a collision. The labour bill comes to £2860. If the mechanics spend 48 hours working on the car, what is the rate for labour per hour?

Answer:

_____

Squaring numbers

QUESTION 1   2 marks

What is 9 squared?

Answer:

_____

QUESTION 2   2 marks

A workshop has an area for a hoist that is 8.2 × 8.2 metres. What is the total area?

Answer:

_____

Ratio

QUESTION 1   2 marks

A driver gear has 20 teeth and the driven gear has 60 teeth. What is the ratio, in the lowest form, of the driver gear to the driven gear?

Answer:

_____

QUESTION 2   2 marks

The ratio of the diameters of driver pulley A to driven pulley B is 1 : 4. If the diameter of driver pulley A is 15 cm, what is the diameter of driven pulley B?

Answer:

_____

Mechanical reasoning

QUESTION 1   1 mark

Pulley 1 and pulley 2 each measure 5 cm across their diameters. Pulley 3 measures 10 cm across the diameter. How many times will pulleys 1 and 2 turn if pulley 3 turns three times?

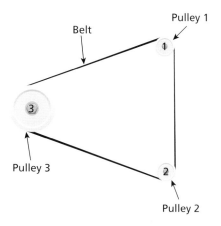

Answer:

_____

QUESTION 2   1 mark

Each gear in the diagram below has 16 teeth which they interlock with each other. If gear 5 turns in an anticlockwise direction, which way will gear 1 turn?

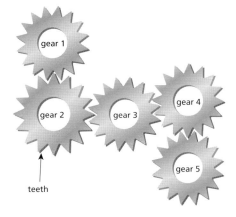

Answer:

_____

Automotive Glossary

Air bag   A safety component fitted to cars that inflates out of the steering wheel and the dashboard to protect the driver and front seat passenger

Alternator   An alternating current generator that has the capacity to change mechanical energy into electrical energy

Bore   The diameter of a hole such as the cylinder of an engine

Brake horsepower   This is the power delivered to the driven wheels

Carburettor   A mechanical device for mixing fuel with air

Chassis   This is the framework of any automobile excluding the car body

Coil   A car component used to increase a battery's voltage to a level that is high enough to jump a spark plug gap

Crankshaft   The main rotating member of the engine. This member changes the up and down motion of the pistons, sometimes known as the crank

Cylinder   The chamber in which the piston moves up and down

Dead centre   This is the highest or lowest position in the crankshaft throw when the piston has stopped moving

Differential   The part of the axle assembly that needs to allow one wheel to rotate at a different speed than the other while transferring power from the driveshaft through to the driven wheels

Distributor   The device that sends the current from the coil to the spark plugs of the engine on older vehicles. This needs to be done in the correct firing order

Exhaust manifold   The section of the engine that collects the exhaust gases from the cylinders and carries the gases to the exhaust pipe

Gearbox   A major unit which multiplies the engine torque (turning force) and provides a means of reversing the vehicle, as well as a permanent neutral

Hybrid   Vehicle using a combination of power sources such as conventional engine and electric motors

Micrometer   A measuring instrument used to measure small sizes. It may have imperial or metric measurements

Thermostat   A component that regulates or operates on temperature change

Transistor   A semi-conductor which can be used to switch electronic circuits and also amplify voltage

Turbocharger   This is a turbine which is driven by exhaust gases, forcing air under pressure into the air intake of the engine, hence increasing the engine's power output

Maths and English Glossary

Adjectives   Describes things, people and places, such as 'sharp', 'warm' or 'handsome'

Adverbs   Describes the way something happens, such as 'slowly', 'often' or 'quickly'

Homophones   Words that sound the same, but are spelt differently and have different meanings

Imperial   A system of units for measurements e.g. pounds and inches

Metric   An international system of units for measurement. This is a decimal system of units based on the metre as a unit length and the kilogram as a unit mass

Nouns   Names of things, people and places, such as 'chair', 'George' or 'Sheffield'

Pronouns   Short words like 'it', 'you', 'we' or 'they', etc. used instead of actual names

Ratio   A way to compare the amounts of something

Verbs   Words to describe what you are 'doing', such as 'to mix', 'smile/frown' or 'walking'

Formulae and Data

Circumference of a Circle

$C = \pi \times d$
where: C = circumference, π = 3.14, d = diameter

Diameter of a Circle

Diameter (d) of a circle $= \dfrac{\text{circumference}}{\pi \, (3.14)}$

Area

Area = length × breadth and is given in cubic units
$\quad$ A = $l \times b$

Volume of a Cube

Volume = length × width × height and is given in cubic units
$\quad$ V = $l \times w \times h$

Volume of a Cylinder

Volume of a cylinder $(V_c) = \pi\,(3.14) \times r^2$ (radius × radius) × height
$$V_c = \pi \times r^2 \times h$$

Times Tables

1

1 × 1	=	1
2 × 1	=	2
3 × 1	=	3
4 × 1	=	4
5 × 1	=	5
6 × 1	=	6
7 × 1	=	7
8 × 1	=	8
9 × 1	=	9
10 × 1	=	10
11 × 1	=	11
12 × 1	=	12

2

1 × 2	=	2
2 × 2	=	4
3 × 2	=	6
4 × 2	=	8
5 × 2	=	10
6 × 2	=	12
7 × 2	=	14
8 × 2	=	16
9 × 2	=	18
10 × 2	=	20
11 × 2	=	22
12 × 2	=	24

3

1 × 3	=	3
2 × 3	=	6
3 × 3	=	9
4 × 3	=	12
5 × 3	=	15
6 × 3	=	18
7 × 3	=	21
8 × 3	=	24
9 × 3	=	27
10 × 3	=	30
11 × 3	=	33
12 × 3	=	36

4

1 × 4	=	4
2 × 4	=	8
3 × 4	=	12
4 × 4	=	16
5 × 4	=	20
6 × 4	=	24
7 × 4	=	28
8 × 4	=	32
9 × 4	=	36
10 × 4	=	40
11 × 4	=	44
12 × 4	=	48

5

1 × 5	=	5
2 × 5	=	10
3 × 5	=	15
4 × 5	=	20
5 × 5	=	25
6 × 5	=	30
7 × 5	=	35
8 × 5	=	40
9 × 5	=	45
10 × 5	=	50
11 × 5	=	55
12 × 5	=	60

6

1 × 6	=	6
2 × 6	=	12
3 × 6	=	18
4 × 6	=	24
5 × 6	=	30
6 × 6	=	36
7 × 6	=	42
8 × 6	=	48
9 × 6	=	54
10 × 6	=	60
11 × 6	=	66
12 × 6	=	72

7

1 × 7	=	7
2 × 7	=	14
3 × 7	=	21
4 × 7	=	28
5 × 7	=	35
6 × 7	=	42
7 × 7	=	49
8 × 7	=	56
9 × 7	=	63
10 × 7	=	70
11 × 7	=	77
12 × 7	=	84

8

1 × 8	=	8
2 × 8	=	16
3 × 8	=	24
4 × 8	=	32
5 × 8	=	40
6 × 8	=	48
7 × 8	=	56
8 × 8	=	64
9 × 8	=	72
10 × 8	=	80
11 × 8	=	88
12 × 8	=	96

9

1 × 9	=	9
2 × 9	=	18
3 × 9	=	27
4 × 9	=	36
5 × 9	=	45
6 × 9	=	54
7 × 9	=	63
8 × 9	=	72
9 × 9	=	81
10 × 9	=	90
11 × 9	=	99
12 × 9	=	108

10

1 × 10	=	10
2 × 10	=	20
3 × 10	=	30
4 × 10	=	40
5 × 10	=	50
6 × 10	=	60
7 × 10	=	70
8 × 10	=	80
9 × 10	=	90
10 × 10	=	100
11 × 10	=	110
12 × 10	=	120

11

1 × 11	=	11
2 × 11	=	22
3 × 11	=	33
4 × 11	=	44
5 × 11	=	55
6 × 11	=	66
7 × 11	=	77
8 × 11	=	88
9 × 11	=	99
10 × 11	=	110
11 × 11	=	121
12 × 11	=	132

12

1 × 12	=	12
2 × 12	=	24
3 × 12	=	36
4 × 12	=	48
5 × 12	=	60
6 × 12	=	72
7 × 12	=	84
8 × 12	=	96
9 × 12	=	108
10 × 12	=	120
11 × 12	=	132
12 × 12	=	144

Multiplication Grid

	1	2	3	4	5	6	7	8	9	10	11	12
1	1	2	3	4	5	6	7	8	9	10	11	12
2	2	4	6	8	10	12	14	16	18	20	22	24
3	3	6	9	12	15	18	21	24	27	30	33	36
4	4	8	12	16	20	24	28	32	36	40	44	48
5	5	10	15	20	25	30	35	40	45	50	55	60
6	6	12	18	24	30	36	42	48	54	60	66	72
7	7	14	21	28	35	42	49	56	63	70	77	84
8	8	16	24	32	40	48	56	64	72	80	88	96
9	9	18	27	36	45	54	63	72	81	90	99	108
10	10	20	30	40	50	60	70	80	90	100	110	120
11	11	22	33	44	55	66	77	88	99	110	121	132
12	12	24	36	48	60	72	84	96	108	120	132	144

Notes

Notes

Notes

Notes

Notes